Flute
Fundamentals
The Building Blocks of Technique

Mary Karen Clardy

EA 730

European American Music Corporation

New York, New York

Contents

Series Editor: Corey Field

© Copyright 1993 by European American Music Corporation

All Rights Reserved   International Copyright Secured   Printed in U.S.A.

Printed on acid-free permanent paper

Edition EA 730   ISBN 0-913574-98-8

Dedication

This book is dedicated to my teachers and to my parents, who were my first teachers. It's difficult to remember where or when a particular skill is mastered, and I owe a debt of gratitude to those who guided my efforts, first as a pianist, then as a singer, and last as a flutist. This book is a compilation of tools gained through practice, performance and teaching the flute for all but the first nine years of my life.

Introduction

It has long been my aim to write a book providing the foundations of flute playing. Daily practice routines build tone and technique essential at every level of flute playing, and through years of personal practice and teaching, I am convinced of the need for fundamentals as the building blocks for the simplest to the most advanced techniques. I use the same basic tools (with variation, of course) that have been helpful to me since I was a young flutist, and I continue to use exercises learned as a student. Although my technical level has advanced from those days, the skills needed are the same. Embouchure flexibility, breath capacity, fluid technique, and physical endurance are the building blocks for every flutist. Experience gained through teaching has made me acutely aware of a lack of these skills, and this book is designed to build foundations for those who practice these exercises. Good luck — practice can be habit forming!

CHAPTER I
Breathing

The most basic of human actions is the ability to breathe, and fundamental to playing any wind instrument is an understanding of the respiration process. Because of the lack of resistance in the flute (as compared to the brass family or other woodwinds such as the oboe or clarinet), quantity and use of the air column becomes our overriding concern. Development of capacity and control of this process is best achieved through exercises which allow the body to exhale and inhale in a normal, relaxed manner. Preoccupation with taking large breaths or holding back the breath while playing often inhibits more than helps the process. Try the following exercises without your flute before beginning practice. You will find that with the breathing system warmed up and ready to go, concentration and physical control are achieved more quickly in your practice session.

Exercise 1

1   Bend over from the waist, allowing your head to remain relaxed and free, look directly back at your knees, and place your hand just below waist.

2   Expel all your air with a strong "whoosh" of sound, feeling contraction in the waist area as you exhale.

3   Inhale deeply, feeling expansion in the waist area, around the back, and throughout the chest as you inhale.

4   Repeat this process at least two more times, and on the last repetition, hold the breath in your body and gradually move to an upright position, retaining the air inside your body.

5   You will feel relaxed, full of air, and ready to begin your playing warmup.

Variation on Exercise 1

Try the same process while standing straight up.   Helpful suggestions include:

1   Keep head and neck free of tension, with shoulders dropped and relaxed in order to take the maximum inhalation.

2   Exhale first, with the same "whoosh" of sound, so that your body is ready to inhale naturally.

3   Inhale, allowing the same expansion in the waist area to occur, and check for this by placing your hand just below the waist to be sure that the abdominal area is moving in and out correspondingly with exhalation and inhalation.

4   Repeat the exercise at least three times in an upright position.

Exercise 1 is designed to expand the quantity of inhalation but playing the flute well also involves release and use of this air. Development of phrasing and control of the air column is best achieved by practicing the next exercise with a metronome.

Exercise 2

With the technique you've just learned for developing quantity of air, now let's try controlling the release of the air column through the flute. Find your favorite middle-register note and play a game with yourself to see how long you can comfortably sustain a note while releasing the air. Use the metronome set at quarter note = 60, sustaining first for four beats, then gradually expanding as far as possible. Keep a chart of your progress and reward yourself after each improvement.

Exercise 3

Learning to take quick, deep breaths is a necessary technique for every flutist, but this can be one of the biggest frustrations of all! The secret to the quick, deep breath is remembering to continue to blow constantly until it's time for the breath. Avoidance of panic before a quick breath will keep the body relaxed, allowing air to flow in quickly, and the next exercise provides practice in developing quick breaths between sustained notes.

↓ = Deep, full breath

|_____ = Constant, sustained air column for the full duration of the note.

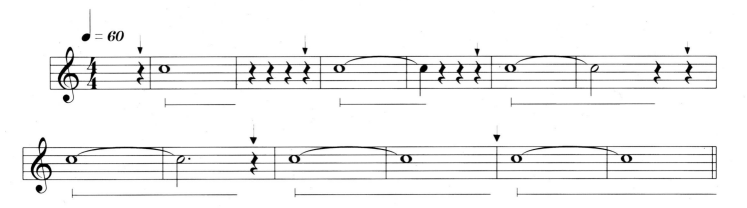

This exercise extends note length while developing skill in reducing the time taken for breaths.

Exercises 2 and 3 may be practiced away from the flute. By concentrating on the air column moving in and out of your body, good physical habits are reinforced before practice begins. Make any sound that you wish (whoo, ssss, tooo, etc.), then repeat the exercise with long tones on your favorite notes.

CHAPTER II.
Embouchure

The EMBOUCHURE, or literally the "formation of the lips" is an essential element for the flutist, helping to control and direct the air column, and a basic description of the shape and position of the lips is as follows:

1 Say the word PURE or POOH, feeling that the bottom lip rolls out as if blowing a kiss or pouting.

2 Keep firm corners, placing them on the canine teeth, for control of the lips and thus the air column.

3 Avoid stretching the lips back against the teeth (as if you were smiling) because this produces a sharp, thin tone and limits flexibility between registers. Although movement will rarely be visible, each register requires a different shape and size of embouchure, changing angle or direction of the air column.

The following illustrations give the general shapes needed for low, middle, and high register.

Low: ⬭
Elliptical shape, with corners back slightly and a more prominent upper lip, direct the air column into the flute.

Middle: o
Rounder shape, moving corners in toward front teeth, make a smaller hole and balance the use of bottom and top lip.

High: o
Roundest, smallest hole, using firm corners to push the lips toward the center, forward and away from the teeth. Lips are used equally and should feel like you are "blowing a kiss."

Other helpful hints include thinking of: Control or "grip" of the air column with the inside (red surface) of the lips rather than with the teeth, jaw, base of the tongue or throat muscles. Creation of a "tunnel" in the lips through which the air column flows from the body into the flute.

Embouchure: Front view

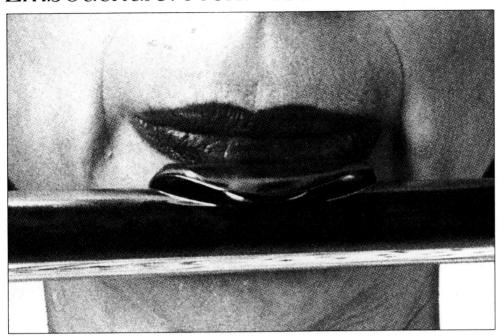

Embouchure: Side view

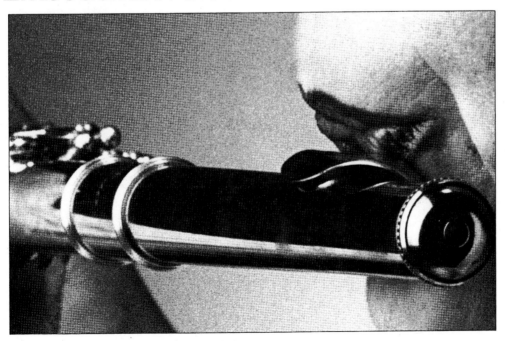

Although embouchure changes are imperceptible when the flute is in playing position, it can be very helpful to practice making the suggested embouchure shapes in front of a mirror without your flute. Watch for size as well as shape of the embouchure in the lips.

Exercises

1 Long tones for embouchure development

Long tone practice helps develop muscle memory in a young player and reminds older muscles what is necessary to produce a good tone at the beginning of a practice day. MM quarter note = 60, use all of your air and concentrate on attacks and releases without bumping the note. Vary dynamics, for example forte, piano, crescendo-decrescendo, or decrescendo-crescendo, and include all registers, particularly focusing on personal weaknesses of control or range.

Then for variety, reverse direction of the exercise, for example:

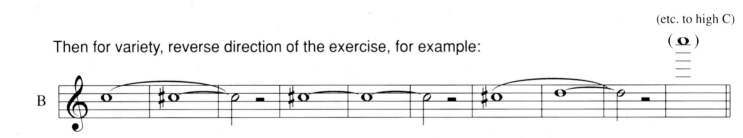

The exercise should be separated into registers (low, middle and high) and practiced at different times. For example practice low register early in the day and high register later in the day, just as an athlete warms up muscles by jogging before sprinting.

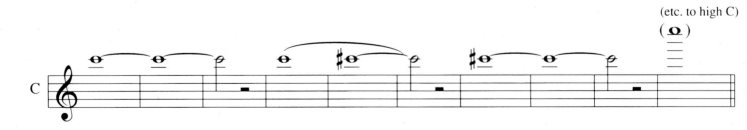

2 Harmonics and octave slurs

Harmonic practice is just as important for the flutist as lip slurs are for the members of the brass family. Although not restricted to using three valves (like the trumpet or french horn), we lack an octave key (contained on the clarinet or oboe) and must use a combination of embouchure and air column in order to produce the overtone series.

Harmonics

Be careful to not force out the upper notes with a bump of air or a tightening in the throat. Remember the embouchure rules given above and think about a subtle adjustment between registers. Practice the entire harmonic series, then practice skipping around, for example 1 3 2 4 3 5 etc. or invent melodies using harmonic fingerings.

After you have mastered the harmonics exercise on the next page, try playing *Mary Had A Little Lamb* on harmonics, first in the key of C, then transpose and play in the keys of D flat, D, E flat, and E:

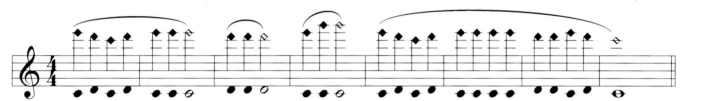

Harmonics

1) Try various combinations (for example 1 3 2 4 3 5 4 6 5 3 4 2 1 or 1 2 4 3 5 4 6 5 3 4 2 1) to develop flexibility and control. You may also begin at the top and practice descending rather than ascending through the series.

2) Always practice harmonics slurred and vary note lengths and rhythms.

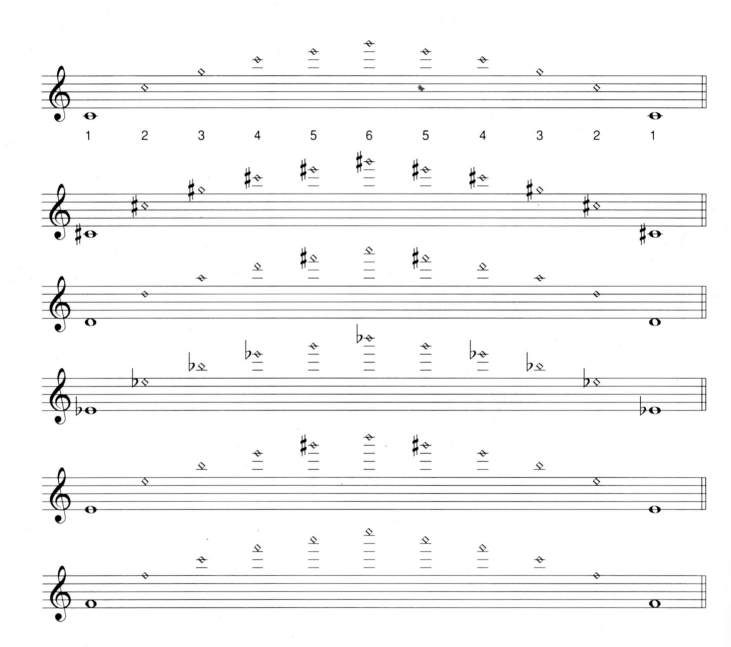

Without completing the top of the harmonic series, practice F# and G in the following way:

Octave slurs

Octave slurs use the same embouchure rules and are also helpful for developing flexibility. Practice octaves, beginning from low to high, then reverse direction, playing high to low. Also work to develop speed and control in octave slurs by practicing with the metronome. Remember to play smoothly without bumping the upper note.

(꜒)
(optional breath for young players)

Continue the exercise using this range of notes:

For variation: 1) Begin on the top note and slur down (i.e. reverse octaves).
2) Try different rhythms.

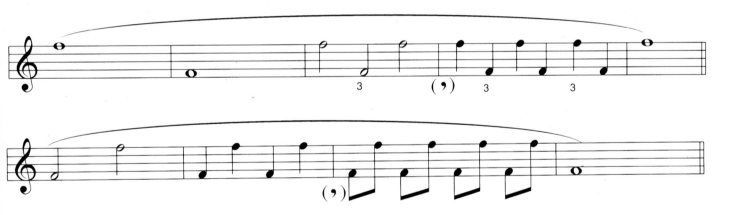

3 Scales in 3rds

These scales should be slurred. Goals for practice include development of smooth finger changes as well as coordination of air column and embouchure.

Scales in 3rds should be practiced with a sense of melody and inflection, following the musical tension and release inherent in a scale. This is another opportunity to practice developing breath control and phrasing. Work to sustain two octaves on a breath, then breathe before descending.

Scales in 3rds

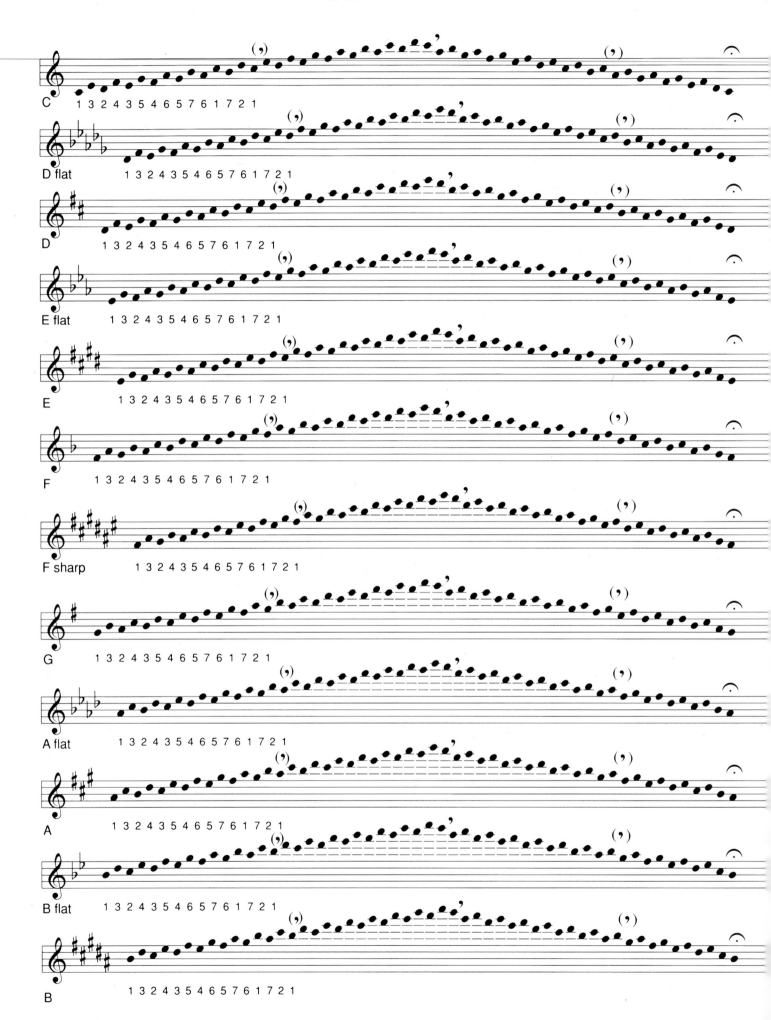

CHAPTER III.
Scales and Arpeggios

Scales and arpeggios are the building blocks of music and should be practiced every day. Listen carefully for the perfect melody contained in every scale. Major scales convey a happy mode, while each form of minor scale (natural, harmonic, or melodic) provides a different flavor of the dark, sad minor mode. Practicing major and minor scales in the twelve keys develops fluid technique throughout the flute and improves sightreading ability. As soon as possible memorize the scales so that you can be free from the restriction of reading. My favorite method of scale practice includes the major and three forms of minor on the same tonic note. Practicing "parallel" minors, rather than the relative minor form, sharpens reaction time when moving from tonic major to minor, a common occurrence in music. This scale exercise also develops breath control and speed in articulation. Practice slurred or with single, double, or triple tonguing. Set personal goals for tempo and breath control, with the ideal being quarter note = 104 for single tongued sixteenth notes, and all four forms of the scale should be done in one breath. Many scale studies are available as a supplement to (but not a substitution for) daily scale practice, and my personal favorites are the Taffanel-Gaubert *17 Daily Exercises*, Reichert, Moyse or Altès studies. Arpeggio practice should include the major and minor forms for every scale.

Scales

Play each scale ascending and descending over a two octave range:

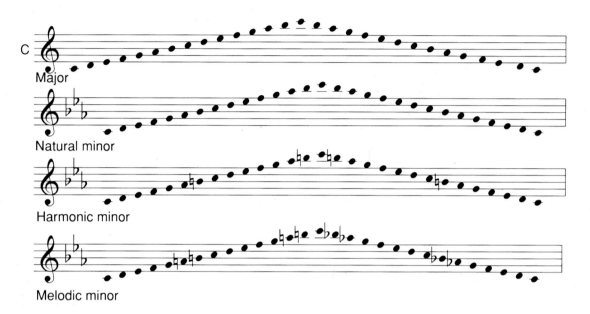

C
Major

Natural minor

Harmonic minor

Melodic minor

1) Practice in eighth or sixteenth notes with the time signature 4/4.
2) Try these various articulations: a] All slurred. b] All tongued. c] Double tongue with straight eighth or sixteenth notes. d] Triple tongued (add one note at top of scale).
3) Also try varied rhythmic patterns:

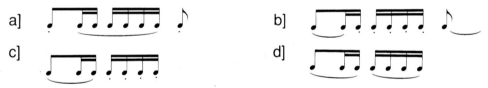

a]

b]

c]

d]

The combinations are endless - so be creative and stretch your imagination!

C#
Major   Natural minor   Harmonic minor   Melodic minor

D

E b

E

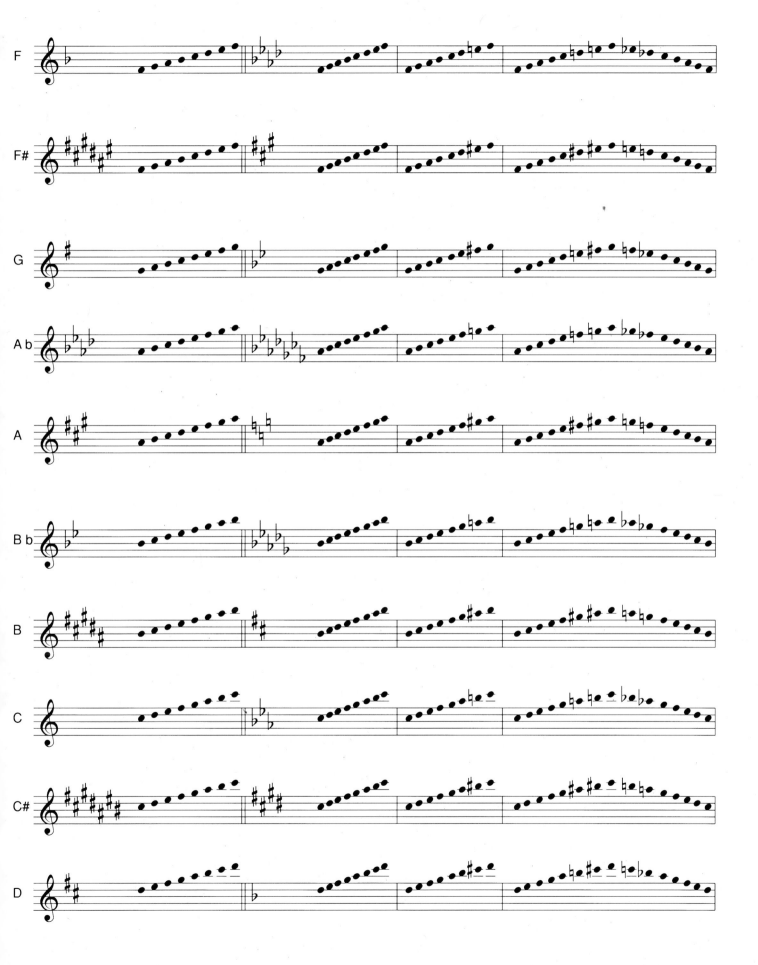

18

Arpeggios

Rhythms should be either 1) straight triplets or 2) ♩ ♫ ♩ ♫

Practice slowly for embouchure development or fast for a technical challenge. Learn to play both arpeggios (major and minor) in sequence on one breath.

CHAPTER IV.
Articulation

The challenge to a flutist when articulating is to maintain a consistent tone quality at all times, particularly in the extremes of register or dynamics, while interrupting the air column through the use of the tongue. Remember to maintain or increase air support and resist the tendency to allow embouchure to open. Use the tip of the tongue with a very light stroke, keeping tongue movement to a minimum, and concentrate on relaxing the back of the tongue when articulating. Articulation on flute should correspond to the various styles of bowing used on a string instrument, from the lightest bounced stroke through a heavier, marcato style, and experimenting with different vowel sounds (oh, ooh, ee) increases the range of possibilities.

Single Tonguing

Place the tongue forward in the mouth, use the tip only and say tooh (in English) or *tu* (in French). Remember to keep air constant behind the tongue, allowing the tongue to feel as if it floats on the air column, and be sure to relax the back of the tongue rather than holding it tight.

Multiple tonguing (Double or Triple) on flute increases our technical ability over the other woodwind family members. Although some single and double reed performers have developed this skill, it is still not common, even in professional performers. Fluid double and triple tonguing are requirements in our repertoire and must be practiced every day. The following exercises are part of my daily routine.

Double Tonguing

Use T and K (with various vowels, ooh or the French "u") at slower speeds and move to D and G for faster speeds. Work at strengthening the second syllable and use a constant air column in order to produce equal tone on both tongue strokes.

Double Tonguing Exercise

For the exercise - Practice, repeating each unit 4 times in order to strengthen the tongue and build endurance. The eighth-rest is used only one time, between the pattern changes in order to come out correctly with the metronome.

Metronome practice should begin quarter note = 120, gradually working up speed to quarter note = 176-184 (without stopping from beginning of the exercise to the end).

Listen carefully to your tone quality and work for the lightest possible tongue stroke.

Triple Tonguing

The three common ways to triple tongue use the T and K syllable in various combinations:

1) T T K   T T K
2) T K T   T K T
3) T K T   K T K

The first two examples are more commonly used by brass players, and most flutists now use the third example, particularly for speed in passages of repeated notes. Imposing triplet groupings on a running double tongue will require practice if you are accustomed to using the first two examples, however the result is well worth the effort.

To develop skill in multiple tonguing, practice the following scales first by repeating each degree of the scale in the *Stationary Triple Tongue* exercise. Then begin articulating scales in double or triplet patterns to develop speed and agility in the *Running Triple Tongue* exercise. Short etudes which focus on multiple tonguing should be memorized and practiced daily.

Double Tongue Practice on Scales

First practice a scale which lies in the middle of the register, perhaps your favorite scale, in order to build confidence and speed. Then try the more difficult ones.

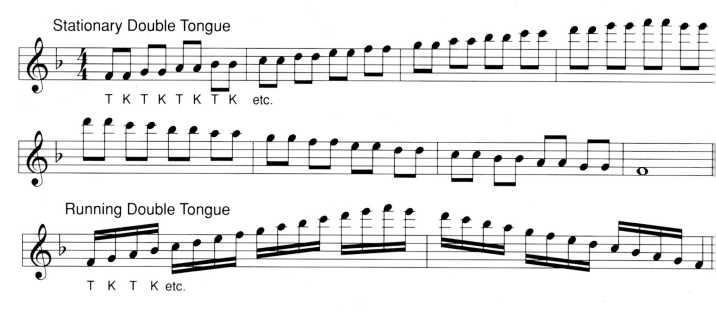

Stationary Double Tongue

T K T K T K T K etc.

Running Double Tongue

T K T K etc.

Triple Tongue Practice on Scales

Stationary Triple Tongue

T K T T K T etc.

or: T K T K T K etc.

Running Triple Tongue

T K T T K T etc.

or: T K T K T K

Etude

for Double Tonguing

Theobald Boehm
from 24 Caprice-Etudes Op. 26

CHAPTER V.
Vibrato

One of the most expressive tools for tone development, projection and phrase shaping is vibrato, defined as a slight variation in pitch in a sustained tone. Production of vibrato in the air column remained a mystery until recent technological advances. The use of a fiberoptic camera, inserted through the nasal passage and suspended at the back of the oral cavity or top of the throat area, clearly shows the involvement of the larynx, and x-rays of singers and wind players show no movement in the diaphragm when vibrato is present in the tone. Without adequate air support, however, vibrato produced exclusively in the throat (commonly known as *"chevrotement"* or nanny-goat vibrato) is undesirable. Vibrato results when a deep, energetic air column passes through a relaxed upper chest and throat, before reaching the resistance created by the embouchure as air is directed into the flute to produce tone. A flutist must learn the proportional relationship necessary for vibrato production in the various registers and at different dynamic levels. Although vibrato should be practiced as an exercise, the result should never sound contrived or planned, and an ideal vibrato should be flexible, following the contours of the musical phrase. Try the following vibrato exercise in order to develop control over the process, and then experiment with your new skill in different musical situations!

Vibrato Illustrations

1 Well modulated vibrato:

Notice that the pitch should be equally above and below the pitch center.

2    Erratic vibrato

3 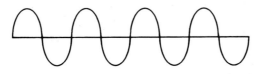   Too wide, particularly at soft dynamic levels or in low register.

4    Too narrow, particularly at loud dynamic levels or in high register.

Practice changing speed and width of vibrato in order to increase variety, control and expressive possibilities.

Vibrato Exercise

This exercise begins as separated notes at a slow speed (dotted-quarter = 60). Pulses should be separate attacks (no tongue) and will feel like a whistle inside the mouth and throat. Be careful not to force the sound! Practice at a mezzo-forte dynamic level.

As you gradually build control and then speed, pulses will naturally run together around dotted-quarter = 76-80. The final goal is dotted-quarter = 112 to 120.

After mastering this register, begin at C and ascend chromatically (exercise B).

After mastering this register, begin at C, ascending chromatically, developing the upper register.

Sonata in F Major
1st movement

Practice this beautiful slow movement when you are first learning vibrato. Concentrate on using vibrato where marked on the long notes. For young students beginning to use vibrato is difficult. Try using a specific number of pulses (for example 5, 6, or 7) depending on the length of the note.

No ornaments are included so you can learn to be creative with this Baroque style.

Carmen Entr'acte

Experiment with vibrato use on longer notes. Try a variety of speeds and widths with different registers and dynamics.

Bizet

CHAPTER VI.
Development of technical skill

Development of technical skill is a combination of daily practice, good hand position, and proper body usage, particularly of the upper body muscles in the back, chest, arms and hands. Remember to warm up cold muscles by practicing slowly at first, and always begin with the familiar territory of scales or technical routines to eliminate added tension. When students begin gaining control of hand muscles during the first two years of study, precise finger movement is often taught by "popping or snapping" the fingers to develop coordination. During the following periods of technical development, however, it's essential that the hand, arm and finger muscles remain relaxed when building speed in technique. If arms, shoulders, hands or fingers hurt during practice, watch out! Serious injuries (such as tendonitis or carpal tunnel syndrome) are frequently aggravated by poor body usage. Breaking up long practice sessions, maintaining your flute in good working order, and listening to your body's signals can prevent damage from occurring.

Good hand position:

Front view:
The fingers are all slightly curved and remain close to the keys. The right hand thumb should be placed under the first finger and stay on the body of the flute, taking care not to allow the thumb to protrude past the edge of the flute. The left wrist is underneath the flute and slightly bent so that the flute rests on the hand, leaving the fingers free to move.

Back view:
The right hand wrist is straight so that motion can travel freely from the arm and through the wrist to the fingers. Notice that the right hand fifth finger is curved and matches the other fingers.

In addition to the exercises given in the preceding five chapters, daily practice should include etudes. My favorite studies include the Andersen *Etudes* (op. 41, 21, 33, 30, 63, and 15), Köhler's *Romantic Etudes* (op. 66), the Karg-Elert *Caprices*, Berbiguier *Études*, Taffanel-Gaubert *Études* (found in the *Méthode Complète*), Altès *26 Selected Studies* and the Paganini *Caprices* (transcribed by Herman/Wummer). In addition to practicing etudes which are difficult for you, it's important to include daily practice of a simpler study, setting the metronome at a challenging pace, playing from beginning to end without pause. Although perfection is ideal, reading through music without stopping for mistakes is essential in developing sightreading ability.

Development of Sightreading Skills

Learning how to sightread correctly saves time and wasted energy, and several simple rules applied before beginning a new etude or piece of music will immediately improve your efficiency.

1   Look at the key and time signatures.

2   Play the appropriate scale and arpeggio, familiarizing yourself with the sound as well as the fingering patterns. Next, check for a change of key or modulation within the piece and play related scales and arpeggios.

3   Visually scan the piece, looking for patterns, either similarities or differences which should be examined before reading.

4   Locate melody and acccompaniment patterns within the music. Practice the melody notes only, eliminating those notes which are connecting "passage work," and develop phrasing as you concentrate on the musical bone structure.

5   Finally, decide on an appropriate tempo so that your eyes move constantly ahead, avoiding stops and starts in the music.

The following Andersen *Etude* (Op. 33, no. 3) has been marked to show suggestions for improved sightreading.

Etude
Sightreading Exercise

Key = G
Time = 9/8
Set MM on the eighth note for sight reading.

M = Melody notes ⌐‾‾¬ = Repeated patterns

Joachim Anderse

Opus 33 no.

Development of Practice Skills

After a first reading, you are now aware of the difficulties and are ready to practice. Just as we have established rules when preparing to sightread, learning specific techniques for practice makes learning faster and easier.

1 Practice with a metronome, setting it at a comfortable speed when learning new material.

2 Articulate each note in slurred passages or add rhythmic patterns in order to smooth out technical difficulties.

3 Practice in front of a mirror, checking for embouchure shape, good body usage and hand position.

4 Record your practice sessions in order to accurately hear the tone quality, intonation, articulation, and technical difficulties. Monitor your progress and reward yourself for improvement.

5 Always practice slowly when learning new music and build tempo by gradually increasing the metronome setting. At the end of a session, practice technical pieces at half tempo. For example if the normal tempo is quarter note = 160 you should set the metronome at quarter note = 80.

6 Don't settle for mistakes! Choose a metronome setting where you make NO mistakes and then develop concentration skills necessary to play perfectly.

7 Memorize! The mental process necessary for memory work builds confidence in performance and is an important skill. Begin with small units, progress to larger sections and then entire movements. Helpful hints include outlining key structure, thematic material, repetitions, and overall musical form.

Practice Skills

Use the following examples, chosen from standard etude books, in order to develop your practice skills, and apply the same suggestions to any new music you begin.

1   Köhler: *In Moonlight,* from *25 Romantic Etudes* Op. 66

2   Andersen: *Etude in E Major,* from *24 Etudes* Op. 15

3   Andersen: *Etude in D Minor,* from *24 Etudes* Op. 15

In Moonlight

From 25 Romantic Etudes

Concentrate on smooth interval connections, especially in wide slurs, and listen carefully for intonation and phrasing in this etude.

Ernesto Köhler
Op. 66 No. 7

This Etude should be used to develop lyric style, practice vibrato skill, and for flexibility between registers.

Etude in E Major

This etude gives practice in developing tone quality while articulating and should be practiced slowly. At the marked tempo, the difficulty of the key and frequency of accidentals makes it challenging for any flutist!

Joachim Andersen
from 24 Exercises, Op. 15

Play also with double tonguing:

Etude in D Minor

Joachim Anders
Op. 15 No.

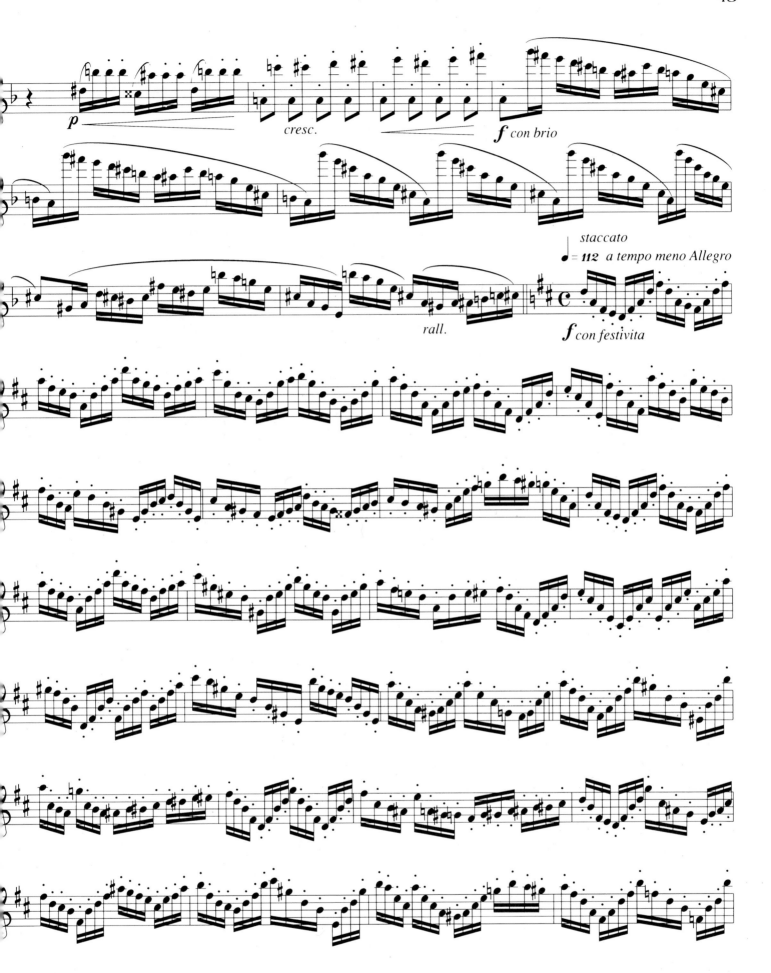